Auguste VESTRIS
1760 - 1842

Dance is as old as mankind, but the earliest recognizable ancestor of ballet was a form of amusement for the court of Louis XIV. These early ballets used mythological and allegorical stories and were performed mainly by men, in masks and elaborately symbolical costumes. From this tradition came Auguste Vestris, the greatest dancer of the famous Vestris dynasty. Born in Paris March 27, 1760, he was the illegitimate son of two dancers--Marie Allard, who excelled in comic and character roles, and finally retired when she grew too fat to dance, and Gaétan Vestris, a great dancer who had been the first to discard the mask. Taught by his father, Auguste made his debut at the age of twelve and was at once acclaimed a prodigy. His first great success was as Amor in his father's ballet, *Endymion;* soon afterwards he was appointed *premier danseur* at the Opéra in Paris --until the rise of ballet in Russia at the end of the nineteenth century the most famous and best paid dancers in the world appeared at the Opéra. In 1778, Auguste danced there in Gluck's *Alceste,* and in the premier of *Les petits riens,* Mozart's only ballet, choreographed by Jean-Georges Noverre, 1727-1810, praised by the actor Garrick as "the Shakespeare of the dance." Gaétan had been hailed as "the god of the dance"; now Auguste inherited the mantle of the first dancer in all Europe. Gaétan acknowledged only Auguste as his superior, declaring, "The explanation is simple, Gaétan Vestris is his father, an advantage which nature has denied me." In vanity they were about equal. Auguste once announced, "In Europe there are only three great men-- myself, Voltaire, and the King of Prussia."

Audiences also admired Vestris enthusiastically. When father and son appeared in London in 1781, Parliament interrupted its session: such dancing had never been seen before. Gaétan was a *danseur noble*, elegant and heroic in style. Auguste, short and knock-kneed, was a *demi-caractère* dancer, excelling in more athletic "character" roles. In 1789 the French Revolution drove Auguste back to London, where for four years he danced with great success in the ballets of Noverre. Noverre had revolutionized ballet, changing it from a plotless interlude to a dramatic form expressing plot and character. Its subjects, however, were still largely derived from mythological and classical themes. In 1793 Auguste made a triumphant return to the Opéra, and remained there until he retired at 56--supremely successful, though often plagued with financial difficulties and once even imprisoned. A dazzling virtuoso, he was particularly famous for his exceptional elevation and his turns: he did things no dancer before him thought possible. In tribute to his range of expression, Noverre called him "the new Proteus of the dance." But not everyone loved him: during a visit to Paris in 1802 Ivan Valberkh, the first native Russian choreographer, complained of Auguste's "grimacing and incessant whirling."

Text by Viiu Menning; art by N. Conkle & D. Neary, with two scenes by G. Barbier

After retiring, Auguste devoted himself to teaching: he was as great a teacher as he had been a dancer. His pupils included the most famous dancers of the next generation: Didelot, Perrot, Bournonville, Taglioni, and Elssler. In 1835 he appeared at the Opéra for the last time, dancing a gavotte with Taglioni. He died in Paris on December 5, 1842. He had been born into an age when the male dancer reigned supreme; when he died the male dancer existed to support the ballerina. His teaching methods had fostered the technical perfection which made possible the Romantic ballet, ironically ushering in a century of the supremacy of the ballerina.

Marie TAGLIONI
1804 - 1884

The first great ballerina in the history of dance was Marie Taglioni. Born on April 23, 1804 in Stockholm, she was the daughter of Filippo Taglioni, a famous Italian teacher and choreographer serving as ballet-master at the Royal Theatre. Filippo gave Marie her first ballet lessons. He remained her principal teacher and mentor throughout her career. He was a relentless taskmaster. Often at the end of a two-hour session Marie collapsed unconscious with fatigue. Yet she submitted to this harsh discipline, for she realized that she and her father formed a perfect team. His rigorous training aimed at molding her into his ideal of a new type of ballerina. Shortly after her eighteenth birthday Marie made her debut at Vienna's famous Kärntnertortheater. She had a considerable success; yet only after another five years did her exacting father judge her ready to appear in Paris, the ballet center of the world, *the* city to conquer.

Taglioni was ready for it. Her debut at the Opéra in 1827 met with great acclaim. Three years later came an equally successful debut in London, in Didelot's *Flore et Zéphire.* Next followed her first major triumph, when she danced in "The Ballet of the Nuns," choreographed by her father for Meyerbeer's opera, *Robert the Devil.* The nuns, robed in white, rose from their tombs to perform an otherworldly dance of graceful, flowing movements. This new style caused an immediate sensation and, indeed, a new verb was soon coined, *"taglioniser,"* meaning to dance with smooth movements.

On March 12, 1832, Taglioni appeared in *La Sylphide* --a turning point in her career and in the history of ballet. With *La Sylphide,* choreographed for Taglioni by her father, the Romantic ballet was born. The two-act work is set in the Scottish highlands --known, from Sir Walter Scott's popular romances, to be mysterious, exotic, and romantic. In the first act James, a young farmer betrothed to Effie, glimpses the otherworldly Sylphide and is fascinated with her. The act is full of local color with stylized Scottish dances, appealing to the Romantic imagination's interest

After a lithograph by A. E. Chalon

Marie Taglioni in *La Sylphide*, Act I

in national differences. The second act appeals to another fascination of the Romantics--the supernatural, often associated with a longing for an unattainable ideal. In a strange forest clearing the sylphides are dancing; James follows his vision here, and seeks to possess her forever. Madge, a witch tells him how, but she is evil, and by following her instructions James kills his Sylphide. Taglioni remained identified with this role throughout her life: in it she introduced the long white tutu (designed for her by Eugène Lamy) --the costume which has since become the visual symbol of the Romantic ballerina. The soft glow of gaslight on the white tarlatan and tulle evoked the characteristically misty atmosphere. In *La Sylphide* Taglioni created a new style of dancing. Her pointe work had previously been merely an occasional trick: she integrated the technique into the ballet. She achieved this before the advent of the blocked toe shoes which make pointe work easier for the modern dancer: her pointe shoes were ordinary ballet slippers, stitched at the toes for greater strength. Taglioni's lightness and fluidity of movement opened a new era in the history of dance.

In the year of this wonderful success Taglioni married the Comte Gilbert de Voisins; the marriage proved bitterly unhappy and the couple finally divorced in 1844, after the birth of a son. But her career remained full of success --and the hard work on which success depended. When Fanny Elssler arrived at the Opéra, rival factions supported these two great dancers, who expressed the two facets of the Romantic ballet. The "rivalry" was most profitable for the Opéra. On September 6, 1837 Taglioni made her Russian debut in St. Petersburg. The event was yet another triumph for her. She danced in St. Petersburg for five seasons, always to full houses and great acclaim, and greatly influenced the development of Russian ballet. After her departure from Russia the inconsolable Petersburg fans held a solemn banquet and consumed a pair of her ballet slippers served in a special sauce. (The term "balletomane" is, predictably, a Russian coinage.) Her farewell performance took place in London in 1847, when she danced in a revival of Jules Perrot's celebrated *Pas de Quatre* and *Jugement de Paris*.

Taglioni retired to Lake Como, where her parents had settled, but this marked the close only of the first chapter of her career. In 1858 the extraordinary promise of young Emma Livry brought her back to Paris. The following year she was appointed *Inspectrice de la Danse* at the Opéra, and in 1860 *Professeur de la classe de perfectionnement*, a post she held for ten years. In this capacity she instituted the system of examinations still retained at the Opéra. In 1860 she created her only ballet, *Le Papillon*, with a score by Offenbach, for Emma Livry, of whom she said, "I never saw myself dance, but I must have danced like her." In the Franco-Prussian war of 1870 Taglioni lost everything; she went to London, where she taught dancing and deportment to children, including royalty. The last four years of her life were spent with her son in Marseilles, where she died April 22, 1884.

Taglioni's contribution to ballet is immeasurable. She altered the course of her art, not only by her technical achievements but, even more, by creating a new style, expressing immaculate and ethereal purity. She introduced into the vocabulary of dance a lyricism, spirituality, and poetic quality which had previously been unknown. Fanny Kemble said that Chopin's music reminded her of Taglioni's dancing, and indeed Chopin was often inspired by Taglioni, who gave form and movement to the dreams of her time.

Fanny ELSSLER
1810 - 1884

Taglioni the Sylphide expressed the spirituality of the Romantics; the other pole of the Romantic sensibility, that which thrilled to the dramatic, the wild, the exotic, found its muse in Fanny Elssler. The greatest contemporary writer on the Romantic ballet, Théophile Gautier, expressed the contrast: "Mlle. Taglioni is a Christian dancer and Mlle. Elssler is a pagan dancer."

"Pagan Fanny" was born on June 23, 1810 in a suburb of Vienna. Her father had been Joseph Haydn's valet and copyist. After Haydn's death in 1809 the family was poor: Fanny and her older sister Therese had to begin earning their own livings as dancers when very young. Fanny's growing success in Vienna soon attracted the notice of Metternich's advisor, old Friedrich von Gentz, who was her companion for two years until his death in 1832. The death of Gentz prompted Fanny to accept an invitation to dance in London, where she made her debut in 1833 at the King's Theatre. Fanny's first two seasons in London brought her great acclaim, and yet, when six weeks after her debut she appeared with Taglioni in *Flore et Zéphire*, the honors went unanimously to Taglioni.

Fanny's Paris debut, cleverly preceded by months of whispered publicity, had been scheduled for September 15, 1834. Taglioni's great artistry had frightened Fanny into lessons with Auguste Vestris, and although the ballet, adapted from Shakespeare's *The Tempest*, was banal, she achieved a great personal success. For the next two seasons she appeared often at the Opéra, usually in variations choreographed for her by her sister Therese. These were often based on national dance motifs, a form which became Fanny's hallmark. Her greatest success in this genre was *La Cachucha*, a Spanish dance she herself arranged and first danced in Paris in 1836, in Coralli's ballet, *Le Diable boiteux*. The *Cachucha* became identified with Elssler, as *La Sylphide* was with Taglioni. Then, after an illness which nearly killed her, Fanny had to struggle to learn to dance again, helped once more by Vestris. In September 1837 at the Opéra she danced for the first time as Lise in *La Fille mal gardée:* the role was one of her greatest triumphs and traces of her characterization

Fanny Elssler
in *La Volière*, after J. D. Francis, 1838

remain in the ballet to this day, especially in the mime. Ten days later she appeared as Fenella, the mute title role in Auber's opera *La Muette de Portici*, and again achieved overwhelming success. Her fame as a great actress-dancer was assured.

After elaborate preparations, including more classes with old Vestris, Fanny embarked for America, where she became the first great ballerina to tour in the New World. After the extraordinary success of her New York debut May 14, 1840 in Coralli's *La Tarentule*, one of her most famous roles, "Elsslermania" set in. All sorts of things were named after her, from boot-polish to cigars, from hats to champagne. Whenever she danced she was greeted with an enthusiasm and generosity unequalled in her European triumphs. A memorized curtain speech became part of her program, and she confided, "If this goes on, I shall really have to learn English correctly." When she danced in Washington Congress adjourned early: no quorum was possible as everyone was at the theatre. In Havana a commemorative medal was struck for her visit. The more she danced, the greater the demand --and the profit: Elssler, an astute businesswoman, always insisted on payment in advance in gold. Her return to France was postponed, her contract at the Opéra broken, and by the time Fanny gave her farewell performance in New York, the one-year trip had extended to just over two years.

The Opéra refused to have her back, but triumphs awaited her in other European centers. She appeared first in London, in *La Tarentule*, to thunderous ovations. On May 30, 1843 she danced in the London premiere of *Giselle*. Perrot had created this masterpiece for Carlotta Grisi, but Elssler made the role her own. She followed this success with a triumphant debut at La Scala in 1844. There remained Russia, and on October 13, 1848, Elssler made her debut in St. Petersburg as Giselle. Taglioni still ruled there, however, and Elssler's reception was comparatively reserved; yet slowly, in such works as *La Fille mal gardée* and Perrot's *La Esmeralda* (also created for Grisi) she won over the St. Petersburg balletomanes. Nevertheless, official delays and intrigues marred her two seasons. She therefore agreed to appear in Moscow, where her debut inspired great enthusiasm. The following season she danced only in Moscow, and met with the greatest success of her career. Her farewell performance, in *La Esmeralda*, on March 2, 1851, was an unparalleled triumph, with 42 curtain-calls and over 300 bouquets. Two days before her forty-first birthday, on June 21, 1851, Elssler danced for the last time, in Vienna, as Marguerite in Perrot's ballet of *Faust*. She had come full circle. After a brief stay in Hamburg with her daughter, she settled in Vienna where she lived quietly, retaining an active interest in the theatre and ballet. She died there early on the morning of November 27, 1884.

The different qualities of Taglioni and Elssler added two terms to the vocabulary of dance criticism. Taglioni was described as a *danseuse aérienne*, of the air, suggesting both her unusual elevation and also the spiritual quality of her art.

Elssler, by contrast, was a *terre à terre* dancer. The term means "down to earth," and refers not only to her quick, sharp technique, but also to the more human, passionate, and sensual appeal of her dancing. Much of her work was in the style known as *demi-caractère*, which means that the dance expressed some individual character or personality. But her greatest achievements were in the ballets of Jules Perrot (1810-1892). Her unique dramatic projection brought his heroines to life, and influenced all future performances. Elssler added to the art of dancing that of acting, thereby establishing new standards of interpretation. Through her dancing she revealed depths of meaning which raised ballet from a pretty entertainment to emotional levels never before imagined.

Fanny CERRITO
1817 - 1909

Young Fanny Cerrito seemed unpromising material for the stage. For one thing, she had heavy features, but by daily massaging she softened them --at least to her own satisfaction. The same kind of tenacity eventually overcame the scruples of the respectable middle-class family into which she was born on May 11, 1817, and saw her placed in the famous ballet school of the San Carlo Theatre in her native Naples. She progressed rapidly, and when she made her debut at the San Carlo in 1832, in a comic ballet, she created an immediate sensation. Triumphs followed in the major Italian opera houses; within a year even the staid Roman audiences were hailing her as "the fourth Grace." In the spring of 1836 she ventured abroad for the first time, to Vienna, where she had her first lessons with the great dancer and choreographer Jules Perrot, who helped polish the natural liveliness of her style.

In 1840 Fanny made her debut in London at Her Majesty's Theatre in the presence of young Queen Victoria. Her success was great, even though London remained devoted to Taglioni. Each was acclaimed for her very different qualities. Fanny's style was marked by rapidity on pointes, alternating with a slow grace in *adagio*. She always concealed the difficulty of the steps by her apparent ease, and carefully controlled her enormous strength. Nevertheless, in that age of frequent encores of especially brilliant sequences, she often fainted on stage. After the London season she danced in the premiere of *La Sylphide* at La Scala in Milan, where the rivalry between the "Cerritisti" and the "Taglionisti" was fierce. But in Rome her supremacy was absolute. After her last appearance there she was presented with a heavily-jewelled coronet. Later that evening some young enthusiasts climbed up to her hotel apartment, smashed her chamber-pot, and scrupulously shared the pieces, which they had set in tie-pins.

But Fanny achieved lasting fame in London. In 1842 Perrot became assistant ballet-master at Her Majesty's, ushering in a brief golden age of ballet in London.

Fanny Cerrito, *pas de l'ombre* in *Ondine*

That summer Fanny danced in his *Alma*, and "Cerrito-mania" gripped London. The erotic appeal of her dancing, coupled with her Neapolitan temperament, conquered the city's fashionable youth. Yet on all her travels she was always strictly chaperoned by her father, a retired soldier who had turned into a typical stage-mother; he was often heard to remark, "We have danced magnificently tonight." Fanny's unassailable virtue was so unusual then as to be regarded as an eccentricity. The 1843 London season saw the peak of her success: Perrot choreographed *Ondine* for her (her partner was Arthur Saint-Léon), and in July, at the express command of the Queen, arranged a *pas de deux* for her and Elssler --the event of the season. Two years later, in compliance with Victoria's wish to see all her favorite dancers appear together, Perrot devised the triumph of his art, the legendary *Pas de Quatre* in which Fanny danced with Taglioni, Grisi, and Lucille Grahn. Perrot repeated his success the following year with *Le Jugement de Paris*, danced by Fanny, Taglioni, Grahn, and Saint-Léon. In July of 1848 Fanny appeared as Spring in the last of his great divertissements, *Les Quatre Saisons*, the only ballerina to dance in all three of these masterpieces --now all lost.

Fanny had been one of the very few dancers to make a name outside the Opéra, but in the autumn of 1847 she finally made her Paris debut. For the occasion Saint-Léon, whom she had married in 1845, adapted *Alma*, renaming it *La Fille de marbre*, and Fanny had another triumph. Some technical weaknesses had always marked her dancing, so the enthusiastic Parisians invented, to explain her success, the new category of *"danseuse de fantaisie,"* as opposed to *danseuse noble* or *de demi-caractère*. Gautier wrote, "she represents the flowering of natural gifts, fantasy and caprice." Naturally, Fanny remains the unique example of this particular category.

Disagreements with a new director led to her leaving the Opéra and going to Russia, but although she was a great favorite with Tsar Alexander II, she had less success with the public. A year later, in the autumn of 1856, she was dancing in the new Bolshoi Theatre in Moscow in *La Fille de marbre* when a piece of burning scenery fell on her shoulder and her costume was alight for several seconds. She was not seriously injured, but the nervous shock of this constant hazard of the age probably contributed to her decision to retire. On June 18, 1857, she danced for the last time, in the minuet in *Don Giovanni*, at London's Lyceum Theatre.

Her dancing was always far better than her acting, but the human quality and the great spontaneity of her movement endeared her even to the most critical audiences. Hans Christian Andersen wrote, "There must be youth, and that I found in Cerrito. It was something incomparably beautiful, it was a swallow flight in the dance, a sport of Psyche."

In retirement she adjusted slowly to the eclipse of her fame, settling down to a quiet, comfortable life in Paris and devoting herself to her daughter by the Spanish grandee Bedmar. She died in Paris May 6, 1909; a few days later the first Diaghilev season opened in Paris, ushering in a new age of ballet.

Carlotta GRISI
1819 - 1899

Carlotta Grisi, last of the quartet of great Romantic ballerinas, was one of the luckiest dancers of all time: the major dance critic of the age, Théophile Gautier, adored her, and the greatest choreographer, Jules Perrot, was in love with her. Born in Visinada, Italy, on June 28, 1819, she entered the *corps de ballet* at La Scala when only ten years old. At this time she was not yet certain whether to become a dancer or a singer; the great singers Malibran and Pasta tried to persuade her to concentrate on her voice. When she was fourteen a tour to Naples decided the question-- she met Perrot and at once became his pupil. In 1836 she made a triumphant London debut, but her debut at the Opéra shortly afterwards attracted little notice. Success in Paris came in 1840 when she appeared with Perrot in a series of character dances; the following year brought her the longed-for prize of a contract at the Opéra. That season she danced in the ballet divertissement in Donizetti's opera, *La Favorite*, with her regular partner, Lucien Petipa. A few months later, on her twenty-second birthday, ballet history was made when Grisi created the role of Giselle.

Giselle was written especially for Grisi by the lovelorn Gautier, who found the story in the works of the great German Romantic poet Heine. The music is by Adolphe Adam. In structure the ballet resembles that other classic of Romanticism, *La Sylphide*, both being divided into two contrasting acts. The first act unfolds in a little village in the Rhineland. Giselle is a happy though delicate peasant girl, deeply in love with Albrecht (created by Lucien Petipa). She doesn't realize that he is a count in disguise. Their love arouses the jealousy of Hilarion, to whom her mother has betrothed her. While Giselle and her friends are performing a light-hearted country dance, Giselle's mother interrupts with an eerie tale of the Wilis, the spirits of young maidens who were too fond of dancing and were betrayed before their weddings; in death they seek revenge by forcing young men who stray into the forest to dance themselves to death. This warning goes unheeded; Giselle is too happy in her new love to entertain any suspicions. A hunting party of nobles arrives and Hilarion contrives to unmask Albrecht, who is already engaged to the Duke's daughter. The shock of this betrayal drives Giselle mad; as the act ends she dies of her grief.

The second act takes place in a mysterious glade at night. Myrtha, the Queen of the Wilis, calls out the spirits. The spirit of Giselle rises from the grave and is ini-

From a lithograph by A. E. Chalon

Pas de Quatre, Marie Taglioni, Fanny Cerrito, Carlotta Grisi, and Lucile Grahn

tiated into the company. Hilarion comes to mourn at Giselle's grave and is caught by the Wilis, who dance him to death. Albrecht also comes, but Giselle intervenes --she dances with him, supporting him through his ordeal until dawn breaks the power of the spirits. Her love and forgiveness from beyond the grave have saved his life. As the ballet ends Giselle disappears with the Wilis, while Albrecht mourns his loss, whose full extent he now feels. The variety and complexity of the title role have earned *Giselle* the reputation of the *Hamlet* of ballets. It remains the greatest ballet of the Romantic period and is still in the repertory of all major classical companies, although present-day performances are based on the Russian, not the original French, version. The choreography was officially credited to Jean Coralli, but it was an open secret that Giselle's solos and *pas de deux* were arranged by Perrot, the first choreographer to make the dancing reveal character and advance the plot. The ballet was at once acknowledged a masterpiece. Grisi's triumph was complete. Gautier decided that she was "Elssler and Taglioni in one person."

Grisi's reputation was now assured. In 1842 she danced in the first London production of *Giselle* and repeated her triumph. She became a great favorite in London and danced there regularly until 1851. In 1844 she created the title role there in Perrot's *La Esmeralda*, again with huge success; the following year she danced in Perrot's *Pas de Quatre*. During this period she continued to dance also at the Opéra, where in 1843 she created the title role in Coralli's *La Peri*, again written for her by Gautier. She danced for the last time at the Opera in 1849, and then went with Perrot to St. Petersburg, where Lucien's brother Marius Petipa, the great choreographer (1891-1910), produced *Giselle* for her. After triumphant appearances in such cities as Vienna and Milan Grisi retired while still at the height of her powers. She was only thirty-four. She retired with her daughter to the country near Geneva and lived in great seclusion and pastoral contentment. Grisi died in Switzerland on May 20, 1899. Her career had brought to her art one of the greatest ballets of all time: she had the privilege of being the first Giselle.

Mathilde KSCHESSINSKAYA
1872 - 1971

Kschessinskaya's life, even when stripped of her own constant improvements on fact, reads like a fairy tale. She was born in Ligovo, near St. Petersburg, on August 31, 1872, and as a child entered the Imperial Ballet School, following the profession of her father, a popular Polish character dancer. After study with such masters as Lev Ivanov (1834-1901: he choreographed the beautiful swan acts of *Swan Lake*) she graduated into the Imperial Ballet. There she advanced rapidly, becoming a prima ballerina within three years. (A ballerina, of course, is not just any female dancer, but a principal female dancer; the prima ballerina is the leading female dancer of the company.) In the small, ingrown world of the company, rife with intrigue and jealousy, her enemies whispered that Kschessinskaya owed her promotions to influence exerted on her behalf. Certainly she had a genius for making powerful conquests: she was the mistress of Tsarevich Nicholas, and when he became Tsar Nicholas II a succession of Grand Dukes took his place as her "protectors." But she was also a virtuosa of rare, exciting brilliance and a great actress. She was the first Russian to master Pierina Legnani's trick of 32 *fouettés* (a whipping series of turns on one pointe), a step still retained in the coda of the Black Swan *pas de deux* in *Swan Lake*. Kschessinskaya achieved a wonderful blend of Italian strength with Russian style; with her, ballet supremacy passed from Europe to Russia. In 1895, only five years after entering the company, she became *prima ballerina assoluta*, the only dancer besides Legnani given this honor.

Kschessinskaya's boundless vitality enabled her to have the best of both worlds. For most of the year she lived for pleasure, her extravagance supported by fabulous wealth; her palace became the center of St. Petersburg's social life. But when the time came for her performance at the Maryinsky Theatre (now the Kirov), a complete change took place. These performances were always clustered at the height of the season, and a month before she submitted herself to a strict regime of long classes and total concentration on her art. Her high-spirited gaiety, dramatic ability, and flawless technique brought her outstanding success especially in *demi-caractère* roles, notably as Kitri in *Don Quixote* and as Esmeralda. When the Italian guest star Carlotta Brianza left, she became the first Russian Aurora in Marius Petipa's *Sleeping Beauty;* indeed, it was Kschessinskaya who convinced the Petersburg balletomanes that native artists could not only equal the Italian stars, but surpass them. In 1904, at the height of her success, she gave her "farewell" performances in *La Fille mal gardée* and *Swan Lake*, "retiring" only to give many performances as a "guest star." When Isadora Duncan saw her dance the following year, even she was filled with admiration, despite her enmity on principle to ballet. Kschessinskaya was adept at the machinations which formed part of life at the Maryinsky, but she was also generous and kind, especially to younger colleagues like Karsavina and Nijinsky-- when Nijinsky graduated into the company, she requested him as her partner, and his fortune was made. At first she intrigued against Diaghilev's ventures, but she eventually danced with his company in London during the 1911-12 season, when she appeared at Covent Garden in the first *Swan Lake* to be seen in the west.

During the Revolution she suffered great losses, endured with courage and cheerfulness: her palace was looted, then confiscated to be headquarters for Lenin, who made speeches from her balcony. In 1920 Kschessinskaya left Russia forever and went to the French Riviera, where she soon gambled away the fortune in jewels she had managed to smuggle out. The following year she became the morganatic wife of Grand Duke Andrei, a mere twenty years after the birth of their son. They eventually settled in Paris, where she opened a school: Margot Fonteyn was among her pupils. At the age of 99, on December 6, 1971, she died at her home in Paris.

Mathilde Kschessinskaya
in *La Fille du Pharaon*

Anna PAVLOVA

1881 - 1931

Even for people who have never seen classical dance, Pavlova means ballet. A legend in her own lifetime, she remains a legend to this day. The facts of her life are clouded by adulatory fiction; even the circumstances of her birth are unclear. She *was* born in St. Petersburg on February 12, 1881, the illegitimate daughter of a poor laundress; but it is highly unlikely that her father was a nobleman, as rumor had it. When she was nine her mother took her to a matinee of *The Sleeping Beauty*, the masterpiece of Petipa and Tchaikovsky, and the magic of the performance so overwhelmed the child that she dreamed of dancing Aurora. She was a frail child but had a strong will, and she insisted on trying for the Imperial Ballet School. With the help of Evgenia Sokolova, who became one of her first teachers, she gained admittance in 1891, despite doubts about her physical weakness. While still at school she attracted notice by her absolute dedication and fine line, especially in arabesque; for a school performance in 1898 the great Marius Petipa revived a curtain-raiser called *The Two Stars* for Pavlova and Michel Fokine (1880-1942). The following year Pavlova graduated into the Imperial Ballet, beginning as a solist and bypassing the hard apprenticeship of the corps. In her third year she danced Giselle, one of her greatest roles, and was acclaimed for the purity and dramatic insight of her performance. She also had a playful side which brought her equal success in character and *demi-caractère* roles, including Lise in *La Fille mal gardée*. By 1906 she had risen to prima ballerina and had danced all the traditional roles but one: two years later she fulfilled her dream by dancing Aurora. The lyricism and youthful grace she brought to the role turned this occasion into one of her greatest triumphs.

Pavlova had little sympathy with the new trends in ballet, but she did work a while with the new young choreographer Fokine. They created *The Dying Swan* for a charity performance on December 22, 1907. This deeply moving solo to the music of Saint-Saëns was born out of only a few rehearsals and Fokine considered it one of his easiest, most natural creations. Its delicate simplicity superbly displayed Pavlova's distinctive poetic quality, her fragility and spirituality, and it will always be identified with her. The previous month she had created the title role in Fokine's *Le Pavillon d'Armide*, with Nijinsky, and during 1908 she created roles in his *Egyptian Nights* and the revised *Chopiniana*, retitled *Les Sylphides*, the first symphonic, abstract ballet, its costumes inspired by engravings of Taglioni. The Romantic nature of this ballet was visually emphasized by the calf-length tutus, a contrast to the usual classical tutu with its short, stiff skirt. That year Pavlova toured abroad for the first time, visiting Scandinavia and Germany with a small troupe. She was on tour also the following year, and did not reach Paris until two weeks after the opening of the historic first Paris season of Russian ballet, brought there by Serge Diaghilev (1872-1929), the great impresario who collected choreographers, composers, and dancers and inspired them to their best work. The most important new works in

Anna Pavlova as *The Swan*
After a drawing by Ivan Bilibin, 1923

ballet came from Diaghilev's company during his lifetime, and most of the generation of choreographers and dancers of importance after his death were survivors of his company. Pavlova joined his troupe and remained until the end of the season, dancing in *Le Pavillon d'Armide*, *Les Sylphides*, and *Cléopâtre* (the retitled *Egyptian Nights*). Her supreme musicality and airy lightness at once conquered Paris, and the Russians were hailed for reviving the art of ballet in the city of its origin.

In 1910 Pavlova made her New York and London debuts, and the next year returned to London, dancing Giselle with the Diaghilev company. Her technique had always shown limitations, but she converted her weakness into strength, blending the ethereal with passionate commitment to each role. Her Giselle prompted the *Times* critic to exclaim, "She is all dance and all drama at the same time." Pavlova lived only for the dance, and when she danced, she did so with her whole being.

These performances were her last with the Diaghilev company. Diaghilev's increasing emphasis on novelty for its own sake conflicted with Pavlova's conservative love of the classics--the ballets she understood, and in which she was unparalleled. In the twenty remaining years of her life Pavlova performed a ceaseless round of tours. She and Victor Dandré --perhaps her husband-- formed a company. Its schedule cut down her appearances at the Maryinsky but she did not finally leave the Imperial Ballet until 1913. She settled in Ivy House in the Golders Green area of London, but was constantly on tour with her company performing primarily the classics, usually in shortened form. Always the audiences clamored for *The Dying Swan;* almost as popular was *Autumn Leaves*, to the music of Chopin, the only complete ballet Pavlova herself choreographed, though she often arranged short divertissements. Much of her company's repertory consisted of pretty trifles, and their banality displeased her, yet she felt she had a mission to bring ballet to all corners of the world, and she did so, despite a very small company and limited finances. Pavlova said, "I want to dance for everybody in the world." She almost succeeded. Frederick Ashton saw her in Peru, Robert Helpmann in Australia, and countless others were similarly inspired by the beauty she revealed at each performance.

Pavlova was the first major dancer to be recorded on film. In 1915 she appeared as Fenella in a Hollywood silent version of *The Dumb Girl of Portici;* it conveys only a vague sense of her dancing but her haunting eyes leave an unforgettable impression. Ten years later Douglas Fairbanks filmed some fragments of her most popular roles, and these suggest a little more of the refinement of her style. But the radiance of her presence eluded the camera. Pavlova died of pneumonia in The Hague, Holland, on January 23, 1931, while on tour. Her unique quality died with her.

What makes a dancer truly great? There are many theories. The famous teacher and dancer Enrico Cecchetti who had taught Pavlova in St. Petersburg and who became the instructor for the Diaghilev company, said, "She possessed that which can only be taught by God." But great dancers are more than inspired performers. They also serve and advance their art. Pavlova embodied quite exceptional heights of perfection while introducing classical ballet to audiences all over the world, thus helping to make possible the present renaissance of dance.

Two days after Pavlova's death, during the second performance presented by the Camargo Society (from which British ballet grew), Constant Lambert conducted *The Dying Swan* in Pavlova's memory. The curtain rose to show a single spotlight playing to an empty stage.

Tamara KARSAVINA
1885 - 1978

Karsavina, the Diaghilev ballerina and favored partner of Nijinsky, was born in St. Petersburg on March 9, 1885. After lessons with her father, a Maryinsky teacher and dancer, she studied at the Imperial Ballet School, graduating into the company in 1902 when she made her debut in a *pas de deux* by the fiery dancer Virginia Zucchi. Her partner was Michel Fokine, with whom she had a youthful romance and in whose ballets she would soon be creating major roles. Karsavina began as a soloist and within only five years was dancing the leading roles in classics like *Le Corsaire* and *Swan Lake*. To her growing fame in such traditional Petipa works she soon added acclaim in new ballets, beginning in 1908 with the revised *Les Sylphides* of Fokine.

Diaghilev's bold vision of a new ballet style attracted Karsavina. She was a member of his company from the first, and when Pavlova was delayed by a tour, Karsavina danced the role of Armida on the historic first night of the Russian ballet in Paris, May 19, 1909. "La Karsavina" and Nijinsky were instrumental in making that season such a phenomenal success. The Parisian triumph brought Karsavina an invitation to dance in London; at the end of the Diaghilev month she began her new engagement, which was extended because of her great success. Thus in 1909 she became the first of the Russian stars to conquer London. The following season, at the Opéra, she created the title role in *The Firebird*, Fokine's first major work for her set to the first major score of Diaghilev's discovery, Igor Stravinsky. Her triumph was complete. She demonstrated her exceptional versatility by appearing also as Giselle, with Nijinsky as Albrecht, but although she won praise, the ballet was not popular with the spectacle-loving public. By now she had also become a prima ballerina at the Maryinsky, but when Diaghilev formed his own company in 1911, she continued with him, that year creating roles in *Le Spectre de la Rose* and *Petrushka*. In the autumn Karsavina and Nijinsky danced *Giselle* in London, meeting the same response as in Paris: the *Observer*'s critic went so far as to pronounce, "it is not a work of art, and can never become one." Her notable new work of the

THÉATRE DE MONTE-CARLO
SOIRÉE DU 19 AVRIL 1911

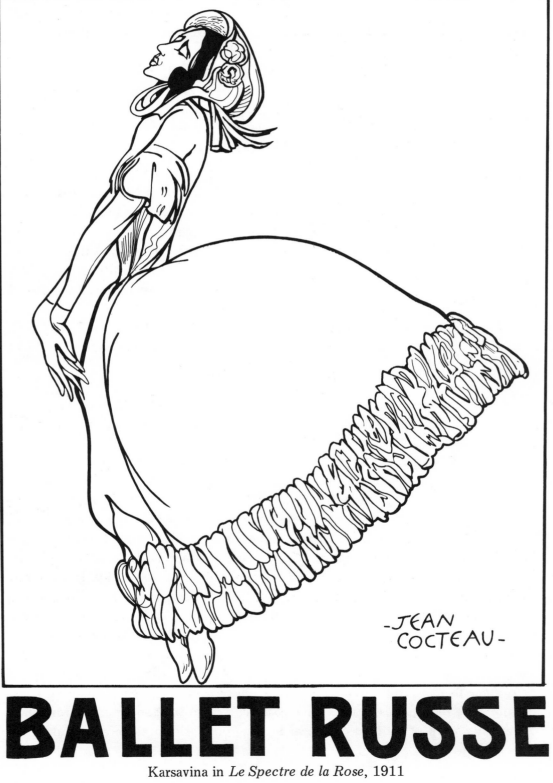

-JEAN COCTEAU-

BALLET RUSSE

Karsavina in *Le Spectre de la Rose*, 1911

1912 season was in *Daphnis and Chloë:* its composer Maurice Ravel coached her himself in the difficult new rhythms. Her remarkably harmonious partnership with Nijinsky was one of the greatest assets of the Diaghilev company, but when Nijinsky was dismissed in 1913 Karsavina remained, later creating one of her favorite parts in Fokine's *Coq d'or.*

During much of the Russian Revolution she was in Petersburg with her second husband, a British diplomat. Although she was president of the newly-formed committee of the ballet, life became increasingly perilous. On May 15, 1918 she danced for the last time at the Maryinsky, in *La Bayadère.* Shortly afterwards she began a harrowing journey to London with her husband and infant son. They arrived safely, and within a year Karsavina created a major role in *Le Tricorne*, the greatest work of Leonid Massine (1895-1979), Diaghilev's new dancer and choreographer. She remained with the Diaghilev company until Diaghilev's death in 1929, then danced with London's Ballet Rambert before retiring.

The list of roles she created for Fokine, Nijinsky, Massine, provides a history of early twentieth-century ballet, but Karsavina was also a superlative classical stylist, especially moving as Giselle. Her contribution to ballet did not end with retirement: she lived in London, becoming one of the founders of the Royal Academy of Dance, and always shared generously with choreographers and dancers her vast knowledge and experience, forming a vital link between the days of Petipa and the modern world of ballet. Undoubtedly she was one of the most intelligent of twentieth-century ballerinas: each role she danced revealed her mind and heart, as does her wonderful memoir, *Theatre Street*, a warm, humorous revelation of the humanity of this greatly-loved prima ballerina. On May 26, 1978 Karsavina died, and an era ended.

Vaslav NIJINSKY
1888 - 1950

Mystery envelops Nijinsky --another legendary name. Even his birth-date is uncertain, for he was born while his parents, Polish dancers, were on tour in Kiev-- probably on March 12, 1888. When his father abandoned the family, his mother managed to enter Vaslav in the Imperial Ballet School in Petersburg. He was a solitary, unpopular student, but his teachers recognized his remarkable abilities, one of them joking about Vaslav's already extraordinary elevation, "The little devil never comes down with the music." He graduated into the company in the spring of 1907, and in his first year at the Maryinsky was dancing with Pavlova in *Le Pavillon d'Armide* and partnering Kschessinskaya and Karsavina. In March, 1908, he danced with Pavlova and Karsavina in Fokine's *Les Sylphides.* Towards the end of

THÉÂTRE DE MONTE-CARLO
SOIRÉE DU 19 AVRIL 1911

BALLET RUSSE

Nijinsky in *Le Spectre de la Rose*, 1911

that year Nijinsky met Diaghilev and began the relationship which changed ballet in this century --indeed, brought ballet into the twentieth century.

In 1909 Diaghilev organized the first Paris season of Russian ballet, opening on May 19 with Fokine's *Pavillon d'Armide*, danced by Nijinsky and Karsavina; the second program included *Les Sylphides*, in which Nijinsky danced with Pavlova and Karsavina. The advance publicity had described Nijinsky as another Vestris; after the first night Paris was acclaiming him as the god of the dance. When an astonished reporter asked him whether it was difficult to stay up in the air so long, Nijinsky obligingly replied, "No, not difficult. You just have to go up and then pause a little up there." These "pauses" of his were a major contribution to the phenomenal success of that one-month season, fitted into the vacation of the Imperial Ballet.

The next summer Diaghilev presented the ballet at the Opéra, where the season opened on June 4 with *Schéhérazade*, in which Nijinsky scored a great triumph as the Golden Slave. Diaghilev also brought back to Paris *Giselle* with Karsavina and Nijinsky, but the public preferred the sensationalism of the exotic new creations. Diaghilev now urged Nijinsky to try choreography, and during 1911 Nijinsky worked on Debussy's *L'Après-midi d'un Faune*. When Nijinsky was reprimanded because a too-short costume had shocked a member of the Tsar's family, he resigned from the Imperial Ballet-- conveniently, just as Diaghilev was forming his own company. In March 1911 Nijinsky left Russia forever; a month later Diaghilev's company gave its first performance, in Monte Carlo. That year Nijinsky created two of his greatest roles, both in ballets by Diaghilev's principal choreographer, Fokine: *Le Spectre de la Rose*, to Weber's music, with Karsavina --an instant success at its premiere in Monte Carlo on April 19-- and Stravinsky's *Petrushka*, first performed in Paris on June 13. The role of the tragic puppet Petrushka was one of Nijinsky's most remarkable triumphs. His technical virtuosity had been acclaimed at once; audiences now recognized his almost uncanny ability to become the character he was dancing, as though, with the costume and makeup, he also put on another being. The success was repeated on the company's first visit to London later that month. Lady Ottoline Morrell summed up his strange power when she described Nijinsky as "a visitor from another world."

On May 29, 1912 Nijinsky made his debut in a new role, that of choreographer, when *L'Après-midi d'un Faune* was first performed in Paris. The ballet created a huge scandal, ostensibly due to a suggestive gesture by Nijinsky as the faun, but more probably because the experimental choreography baffled a public accustomed to a less intellectual form of novelty from Diaghilev. The following year Paris saw the premiere of Nijinsky's second ballet, *Jeux*, which was also misunderstood and unpopular. In the same month came the first performance of his third work, *Le Sacre du printemps*, to Stravinsky's revolutionary music, and this time a riot broke out in the theatre; both the score and the choreography provoked outrage, and wits called the work the "massacre."

G Barbier

Vaslav Nijinsky in *Festin*, 1909

At the end of this eventful summer the company sailed for a tour in South America, without Diaghilev. During the long crossing a persistent Hungarian corps dancer called Romola de Pulszky got herself engaged to Nijinsky, and they were married in Buenos Aires on September 10, 1913. While Diaghilev was now involved with Leonid Massine, he considered Nijinsky a traitor, and dismissed him from the company. Nijinsky formed his own company, a venture which failed quickly. World War I led to his internment in Budapest until February 1916 when pressure by world leaders released him, to rejoin the Diaghilev company, now in New York for their first American tour. On April 12, 1916, Nijinsky made his debut at the Old Met, in *Spectre* and *Petrushka*, and conquered New York. There on October 23 he presented his last ballet, *Till Eulenspiegel*, to Richard Strauss's music. This work was a great success. Nijinsky was the idol of the New World. After a charity performance in New York, society ladies stole most of his underwear for souvenirs. A coast-to-coast tour followed, and in 1917 another tour of South America, during which he danced for the last time with the Diaghilev company, at the age of twenty-nine.

The remainder of Nijinsky's life is a story of tragedy and heroism. His last tour was followed by a winter of idleness at St. Moritz. Perhaps his enforced isolation from ballet brought on his breakdown --he felt he could no longer continue with Diaghilev mainly because he wanted to create ballets, and Massine had replaced him as the new choreographer --but soon he was diagnosed as an incurable schizophrenic. In January of 1919 he gave a private performance at a hotel in St. Moritz, and this last performance was a terrifying mixture of genius and insanity. After years in hospitals he was allowed to return to the care of his wife, who had never lost hope; now World War II caught the couple. They experienced incredible danger and hardship in Hungary and then Austria, but acts of great kindness helped them survive and enabled them in 1947 to settle in England. On April 8, 1950 Nijinsky died in London. But he was not to find rest yet, for in 1953 his remains were moved to Paris, to the cemetery of *Sacré Coeur*, where he lies with Auguste Vestris, Théophile Gautier, and Emma Livry.

Nijinsky was not only the greatest male dancer of all time, although his exceptional technique and instinctive dramatic gift, his supreme musicality and flowing line assure him of that position. It was said that when he executed one of his amazing leaps, he seemed to come down more slowly than he rose. He was also a major innovator in choreography. Although all but one of his ballets are now lost, his sister Bronislava Nijinska (1891-1972) carried on his experiments and saw his style gain acceptance. During the brief decade of his career Nijinsky revolutionized ballet in both areas.

There is an abundance of fact about him, yet nothing is really known or understood; Nijinsky remains an enigma --a genius.

Olga SPESSIVTSEVA

Born 1895

With hindsight the tragedy which befell Spessivtseva seems inevitable. She was born July 18, 1895 in Rostov into a prosperous family. Her father died while she was very young and extreme hardship followed, even a period in an orphanage. At the age of ten Olga was admitted to the Imperial Ballet School in St. Petersburg where at last she found order and security--always a need for her. She was a dreamy, withdrawn pupil, but she was absolutely dedicated and progressed brilliantly. She entered the Maryinsky in 1913 and at once received solo roles. Her impeccable classical style and ceaseless striving for perfection made her one of the company's most admired ballerinas.

Although her conservative taste made her suspicious of Diaghilev's innovations, she agreed to replace Karsavina on his company's first U.S. tour in 1916; there she danced *Spectre de la Rose* and *Les Sylphides* with Nijinsky. But the classics and the Maryinsky were her home. By 1918 she had become a prima ballerina, and the following year she made her debut as Giselle. Memories of Pavlova were still vivid, but the flawless technique and extraordinary pathos of Spessivtseva's interpretation won her an unqualified triumph. She was born to dance Giselle-- and to live the role. Her frailty added to the effect she created, but almost brought her career to an end, for the deprivations of the Revolution gave her tuberculosis. By 1921 she was able to resume dancing, and that year she made her London debut in Diaghilev's splendid, ill-fated production of *The Sleeping Princess*, dancing Aurora on opening night. The delicacy and purity of her performance won great praise, but the season failed financially and she returned to Russia, where she soon repeated her success as Aurora. In 1924 she finally left Russia and accepted a contract at the Opéra, where she remained as *étoile* (star) until 1932, although with many interruptions--she was often at odds with management. She rejoined Diaghilev's company briefly and in 1927 created the title role in Balanchine's *La Chatte*. Back at the Opéra she had an unexpected success in a revival of Guerra's *Salomé* and also appeared in the first performance of the Balanchine/Lifar *Creatures of Prometheus* to Beethoven's music. But it was in the classics that she excelled, and it was because she was given the second act of *Swan Lake* to perform that she danced at Covent Garden with Diaghilev's company in 1929. Diaghilev's death that summer shattered her, ending all hopes of the great *Giselle* he had planned to produce for her. After leaving the Opéra, Spessivtseva did dance in a great *Giselle*, the historic 1932 performances at the Savoy Theatre organized by the Camargo Society, heralding the revival of classical ballet in England.

Her increasingly fanatical perfectionism caused her to reject several contracts and she did not dance again until 1934, when she toured Australia. Again she faced glowing memories of Pavlova, but the tour was the greatest triumph of her career--

Olga Spessivtseva in the Mad Scene, Giselle, Act I

Paris Opéra, 1932

that is, until the first signs of mental breakdown compelled her to leave the company. She gave her farewell performances in Buenos Aires in 1937 and then retired to Paris. The imminent war brought her to New York, but the confusion of the new life and absence from the art for which she had sacrificed everything caused her a severe breakdown in 1940. Until 1963 she was in a state mental hospital, not recognized as a great ballerina, believed dead by many of her colleagues. She had been declared incurable, but after more than twenty years the horror passed and, largely through the efforts of Anton Dolin, she was released. She now lives on the Tolstoi Farm in upstate New York.

Spessivtseva was one of the greatest of all classical stylists and the finest Giselle of her time. Her devotion to her art was total, even extreme. Of her Giselle it was said, "She danced not for herself, not for an audience, but for the Dance itself." But she could not separate the dancer from the dance.

Alicia MARKOVA
Born 1910

Alicia Markova was born Lillian Alicia Marks, on December 1, 1910, in north London. She had a weak knee: the doctor recommended a brace, or perhaps some "fancy dancing" might strengthen the knee. The child chose "fancy dancing" and quickly revealed an amazing aptitude. At the age of ten she made her first professional appearance--in a pantomime billing her as "LITTLE ALICIA--THE CHILD PAVLOVA." Alicia now began to study with Princess Serafine Astafieva, in whose studio she first met and danced with Patrick Healey-Kay (1904-   ), who became her famous partner Anton Dolin. From the start her technique was phenomenal. Diaghilev was so impressed that he planned to add a role for her in his famous production of *The Sleeping Princess.* Now came her first bitter disappointment: she caught diphtheria and was unable to take the part. However, the great Diaghilev's attention made her realize that she wanted to become a dancer.

The following year, when she was twelve, she danced *The Dying Swan* at the Royal Albert Hall, and the critics remarked on her great similarity to Pavlova. But in the twenties there was no outlet for her talent in Britain. She needed to join a company. Astafieva arranged for her to dance before a now-reluctant Diaghilev. At the end of her short performance Diaghilev exclaimed to Astafieva, "You have given a genius to the world. The ballet has found its next generation." And he at once Russianized her name. On her fourteenth birthday Alicia was accepted into his company, where she remained for four and a half years, until the devastating blow of Diaghilev's sudden death. Ballet in the West seemed to collapse, but Alicia's loss was especially great, for he had been a second father to her; she had called him "Sergypop," and a special bond had united the great impresario and the youngest member of his company.

The next two years brought very little work; it was a period of hardship and discouragement for the promising ballerina. But those years saw the beginnings of British ballet. The Ballet Club was formed, and Markova danced at the first performance, on February 16, 1931. The ballet, *La Peri*, had been specially created for her by a young choreographer named Frederick Ashton (1906-   ). The Club had enthusiasm and talent, but no money; they performed only on Sunday evenings. Ninette de Valois (1898-   ) now tackled the redoubtable Lillian Baylis, who managed the Old Vic and Sadler's Wells, and proposed that ballet as well as opera be presented at the Sadler's Wells Theatre. The Vic-Wells Ballet was formed, soon to be known as the Sadler's Wells Ballet.

Early in 1932 Markova danced with the new company for the first time. She was an instant, overwhelming success. Her immense personal popularity contributed to establishing the company and ballet in Britain--audiences came to see *her*, and gradually acquired a love of the art. From the autumn of 1933 until May 1935 Markova was the company's prima ballerina. The great classics were mounted for her and it was at the Wells that she first danced them complete. When Nicolai Sergeyev revived *Giselle* for her, he gave her detailed coaching on how the ballet had been danced in Petersburg and Spessivtseva added her guidance. On New Year's Day 1934 Markova danced Giselle with Dolin--the first time the ballet had been presented with British dancers: it was a triumph. Four weeks after this historic performance Markova danced in the first complete production of *The Nutcracker* seen outside Russia.

Although Markova was supremely a classical dancer, she demonstrated her great range by creating roles in many new works, notably in *Les Rendezvous*, Ashton's first ballet for the company, and in de Valois' *The Rake's Progress*, the first all-British ballet. Markova's last night with the company aroused such enthusiasm that three taxis were needed to take home all the flowers.

The next stage in Markova's career again furthered British ballet. With Anton Dolin she founded the Markova-Dolin Ballet; for two years this all-British company toured throughout England with a varied repertory of modern works and extracts from the classics. Markova's rare versatility and extraordinary presence, and, especially, her uniquely harmonious partnership with Dolin, increased the public demand for ballet. Performances were invariably sold out, yet the company lost money and had to be disbanded. There followed a rather difficult period with the Ballet Russe de Monte Carlo, but she did create roles in several works by Massine. Serge Lifar (1905-   ) was often her partner, but when they danced *Giselle* at London's Drury Lane Theatre his extremely unprofessional jealousy of her triumph caused a minor scandal. A few months later the company visited New York where

Alicia Markova in *Giselle*, Act II

on October 12, 1938 Markova made her debut at the old Met. The ballet was again *Giselle* and again was almost ruined by Lifar's ungallant attempts to steal scenes, but Markova had a great personal triumph. In 1941 she joined the Ballet Theatre (now the American Ballet Theatre) and during the next four years toured the length and breadth of the U.S., bringing ballet to cities and towns which had never before seen it. Everywhere her artistry and magnetism won enthusiastic followers. After the war she made a triumphant return to London, followed by ceaseless tours throughout the provinces. In 1950 London's Festival Ballet was formed around her. Both with that company and as a guest artist she continued to dance all over the world. Her range encompassed works created for her by the major choreographers of our time, but, above all, she was an outstanding classical stylist. Her interpretation of *The Dying Swan* proved her a worthy successor to Pavlova, whom she closely resembled. But the role which remains her triumph is Giselle, the ballerina's Hamlet. The subtle insight of her characterization and her flawless technique have made her Giselle legendary. Similarly her partnership with Dolin set standards by which *pas de deux* must henceforth be judged. She retired in 1962 at the height of her powers and with undiminished popularity. The following year she was a "Dame of the British Empire" for her extraordinary services to British ballet--indeed, world ballet.

True to the traditions of her art, since retirement Markova has devoted herself to transmitting her knowledge to new generations of dancers, linking the days of Diaghilev and Cecchetti to the present. For six years she was ballet director at the Met and since 1971 she has been a visiting professor of ballet at the University of Cincinnatti. Recently she directed *Les Sylphides* for the Festival Ballet, drawing on her experience with Fokine to recreate successfully the atmosphere of this most delicate ballet.

When Markova was born, north London was the last corner anyone would expect to be the birthplace of a great ballerina. It was necessary at least to seem Russian to be taken seriously as a dancer. She changed all that. Her artistry won international acceptance and acclaim for British dancers and helped establish ballet in Britain. She is the first British ballerina in history.

Galina ULANOVA

Born 1910

Ulanova, who was born to dance, at first didn't much want to. She was born in Petersburg on January 8, 1910; her parents were both dancers with the Imperial Ballet there. Early lessons from her mother, a noted teacher, overcame Galina's tomboy reluctance, and she completed her training with Agrippina Vaganova, one of the most important teachers of this century, whose system remains the basis of much teaching today, especially in the U.S.S.R. In 1928 Ulanova graduated into the company, soon appearing in all the traditional ballerina roles. Within two years she was adding to her classical repertory the leading roles in contemporary Soviet ballets.

Ulanova's unique qualities first shone forth in 1934 when she created the role of Maria in Zakharov's ballet *The Fountain of Bakhchisarai*, inspired by Pushkin's poem. This work not only started the Soviet fashion for ballets on literary themes but began the emphasis on characterization through techniques of the famous Stanislavski method. Ulanova's Maria was an extraordinary triumph of acting in dance. Plans were now made for a ballet of *Romeo and Juliet*. Serge Prokofiev composed his renowned score with Ulanova in mind, but when he completed it the Kirov (the old Maryinsky, renamed to honor an assassinated Bolshevik leader) rejected it as too difficult to dance. A Czechoslovakian company had the honor of presenting the first production; not until January 11, 1940 was *Romeo and Juliet* seen on the Kirov stage. The Kirov had been wrong: the ballet was a masterpiece. Dancing with her regular partner, Konstantin Sergeyev, Ulanova created in Juliet a character of radiant humanity and deep pathos. Her dramatic projection won her acclaim as ballet's "supreme realist." Stanislavski said, "She speaks to the mind and moves the heart in her dancing."

During the siege of Leningrad the Kirov company was evacuated to Perm; afterwards, Ulanova was transferred to the Bolshoi in Moscow, with whom she had danced often since 1935. With the Bolshoi she repeated her triumphant Juliet and, five years after joining the company, created the leading role in Lavrovsky's new version of *Red Poppy* in 1949. Five years later she achieved a tremendous success when she created Katerina in Lavrovsky's *Stone Flower*, one of the most popular of Soviet ballets. Again Prokofiev composed the music with special regard for Ulanova's remarkable musicality and expressive range. Indeed, Prokofiev's third major ballet score, *Cinderella*, was also composed for Ulanova, although she didn't create the role.

Ulanova continued to dance traditional roles too, bringing to such works as *Raymonda, La Bayadère,* and the popular Russian favorite *The Little Hump-backed Horse* the same dramatic insight and commitment which distinguished the roles she created. In 1945 she first danced in the West, and she headed the famous company on its historic first visits to London (1956) and New York (1959). To Western audiences she revealed a warmth of interpretation and lyrical delicacy which seemed superbly Russian. After 1959 she limited her performances, and in 1962 came the emotional evening of her farewell.

A chapter in the history of Soviet ballet had ended. But not altogether, for Ulanova has remained with the Bolshoi as ballet-mistress and coach, passing on her knowledge to younger dancers, especially to her protégée, the great Yekaterina

Galina Ulanova as *The Dying Swan*

Maximova. Films give some idea of Ulanova's unique sympathy and gentleness of characterization; in 1954 she danced in a complete *Romeo and Juliet* and three years later was filmed as Giselle and in her version of *The Dying Swan*. But the true legacy of this great dancer lives in the memories of those who saw her and in the new generation of Bolshoi dancers, to whom she hands on the continuous tradition of her art.

Margot FONTEYN
1919 - 1991

Fonteyn's timing has always been flawless. She grew up to international greatness with the young Sadler's Wells Ballet; it gave her the opportunities to develop her artistry. She in turn, by inspiring the company's great choreographer, Frederick Ashton, and by enabling the company to present the masterpieces of ballet with a true prima ballerina, helped the young group of dancers grow into the Royal Ballet.

She was born Margaret Hookham, in Reigate, Surrey, on May 18, 1919. Dancing lessons began as an aid to deportment and, when her father, an engineer, was sent to China, continued in Shanghai with George Goncharov. When she was fourteen it was time to decide whether she was good enough to become a dancer, so her mother took her back to London and she began lessons with Astafieva. This great teacher, who had taught Markova and Dolin, first fired the child with enthusiasm for dancing as a serious art. The following year Fonteyn entered the Sadler's Wells school. The company was very small and pupils were needed to fill out the large ballets. Thus within a few months Fonteyn made her debut in *The Nutcracker*-- as the third snowflake in the second group on the left. When the curtains closed after that first performance the spell of the theatre had already wound its way into the tiny snowflake's being and there was no going back.

The next year, 1935, was a turning-point for both Fonteyn and the company--their fortunes were to be interwoven from now on. The eventful year began with Fonteyn's first principal part, in *Rio Grande*, dancing the role Ashton had created for Markova, Fonteyn's great ideal. Then Markova left to form her own company with Dolin, and Ninette de Valois, the company's far-seeing director, began grooming Fonteyn as her successor. Soon Fonteyn danced Odette for the first time, but not yet Odile; another two years were to pass before she was ready for the complete *Swan Lake*. In 1935 also Fonteyn created her first major role, in Ashton's *Le Baiser de la Fée*. The collaboration between choreographer and dancer was perfect and was to result in the distinctively English style, marked by supreme musicality, purity, and emotional insight.

Two Ashton creations followed in 1936, setting the seal on this rare and fruitful relationship: *Apparitions*, with Robert Helpmann, beginning the first of the three remarkable partnerships in Fonteyn's career, this one lasting for fourteen years; and *Nocturne*. During the next season Fonteyn created yet another role for Ashton, in his witty ballet, *A Wedding Bouquet*. That year, at the age of seventeen, she danced her first Giselle and, as de Valois said, "had greatness thrust upon her." In December came her first complete *Swan Lake*--within three years of her admission as a pupil. The rapid advance occurred because the company needed a ballerina; under de Valois's expert tutelage, the need created a ballerina.

When Diaghilev's *Sleeping Princess* failed so expensively in 1921, he remarked that he'd merely been fifteen years ahead of the time. De Valois agreed, and now prepared to mount the ballet for Fonteyn. This was the first production undertaken by the West. The prospect terrified Fonteyn. For *Giselle* and *Swan Lake* she had had the glowing example of Markova to draw on, and Karsavina herself had coached Fonteyn in some details of *Giselle*. But none of this was available to help create the character of Aurora. The frightening challenge turned into an outstanding triumph. In February 1939 Fonteyn simply became Aurora. For a quarter of a century she was the role's supreme interpreter and it remains identified with her. Her Aurora was the dawn, the essence of youth and joy, unbearably touching in the fragility of these fleeting qualities, which Fonteyn alone could bring to life and motion.

Then the outbreak of World War II shook the young company. The men were drafted, conditions were hazardous, materials for mounting ballets were almost non-existent, but the company struggled on. They toured Holland in 1940, just as the Germans invaded; somehow de Valois managed to evacuate her charges, and only sets and costumes were lost. That year Ashton created his tragic masterpiece, *Dante Sonata*, danced by Fonteyn and Helpmann; then he was called into service. Helpmann, an Australian, alone remained. In 1942 he created *Hamlet*, in which Fonteyn danced Ophelia. During the war years *Coppélia* was added to Fonteyn's repertory and revealed her wonderful comic talent.

On February 20, 1946, *The Sleeping Beauty* shone forth on the stage of the Royal Opera House, Covent Garden. During the war the famous theatre had been used as a dance-hall. This performance marked the dawn of a new era in the history of the theatre and of the company, which now took up residence there. Fonteyn's smiling Aurora was the brightest symbol of the awakening after the darkness of the bitter war years. A few months later Fonteyn created a role in Ashton's abstract masterpiece, *Symphonic Variations*, an unparalleled expression of clarity and lyricism set to César Franck's music. Ashton's first full-length ballet, *Cinderella*, was also created for Fonteyn but a serious injury prevented her from dancing in the opening performances in 1948. She had recovered by the following year, when she danced Aurora during the company's first visit to the Met. The New York

Margot Fonteyn as Princess Aurora
in *The Sleeping Beauty*

audiences responded with such warmth that the dancers were completely bewildered. Fonteyn and the Sadler's Wells Ballet conquered the city, which fell under the spell of Fonteyn's smile. The old image of the tragic ballerina yielded to the new vision of youth and happiness embodied in the young ballerina whose unaffected personality flowed so effortlessly across the footlights.

In 1951 Fonteyn began to dance with a new partner, the cool, handsome Michael Somes. For them Ashton created another magnificent work, *Daphnis and Chloë*. Although Fonteyn is undoubtedly the supreme "Ashton ballerina," her versatility has brought her equally great acclaim in the works of other choreographers, notably in the uncharacteristic role of the Firebird in Fokine's classic ballet, mounted in 1954; Karsavina coached her. That same year Fonteyn became the second president of the Royal Academy of Dancing. 1956 was a year of accolades: by Royal Charter the company de Valois had founded twenty-five years before became the Royal Ballet, and Fonteyn became Dame Margot, the first ballerina so honored while still at the height of her career. Indeed, many of her greatest achievements were still to come. Not until two years later did she create the title role in Ashton's *Ondine,* a work she describes in her *Autobiography* as her "happiest" ballet and one which will always be identified with her. Throughout this period she appeared as guest artist all over the world, as she continues to do.

During the first Royal Ballet tour of the U.S.S.R., in 1961, Fonteyn heard rumors of an extraordinary Kirov dancer who'd just reached the West. Soon afterwards he danced at a charity Gala she was organizing and Fonteyn met Nureyev. The most exciting ballet partnership of our time was born in February 1962 when Fonteyn and Nureyev danced *Giselle* at Covent Garden. Fonteyn has always excelled in *pas de deux*. Her gift for evoking a relationship with her partner involves the audience completely in the movements on stage. It is impossible to watch Fonteyn without caring intesely about the character she becomes. Ashton perfectly captured the power of the new partnership in *Marguerite and Armand*, created for them a year after their famous *Giselle*. Kenneth MacMillan's version of *Romeo and Juliet*, although not created for them, brought one of their most moving triumphs when they danced at the first performance in 1965. The most recent creation of this unique partnership was Ashton's *Hamlet Prelude* (now called *Hamlet with Ophelia)*, especially choreographed for the Silver Jubilee Gala at Covent Garden on May 30, 1977. Fonteyn goes from triumph to triumph, an inspiration to the whole world of ballet and all who share her love of the art.

When Fonteyn was about six, she saw a poster advertising a performance by Pavlova. In answer to her question, her mother told her that Pavlova was the greatest dancer in the world. The child thought for a moment and replied, "Then I'll be the second greatest." She is that--at the very least.

Maria TALLCHIEF
Born 1925

Maria Tallchief's remarkable career included a series of important "firsts": she was the first "Balanchine ballerina" and the first American ballerina to win international recognition. Tallchief is truly American: her father was American Indian and her mother of Scotch-Irish descent; she was born on the Osage reservation in Fairfax, Oklahoma, on January 24, 1925. When she was eight the family moved to Los Angeles, where Maria received her first real lessons, studying with Bronislava Nijinska and David Lichine. She was also a gifted pianist and during her teens felt torn between these two careers. The dilemma was solved when in 1942 she was asked to join the New York-based Ballet Russe de Monte Carlo, enabling her to study at the School of American Ballet. War-time passport quotas delayed some of the European dancers in Europe, so Maria joined the company on tour in Canada and danced small roles within months of becoming a member. As a soloist she attracted notice, and in Montreal won acclaim in Nijinska's *Snow Maiden* as Spring, a role created for the company's prima ballerina, Alexandra Danilova. Her first created role followed quickly, for Agnes de Mille was so struck by Tallchief's style that she added a small part for her in the ground-breaking *Rodeo*, first performed at the Met on October 16, 1942. From now on Maria Tallchief and the history of U.S. ballet become linked.

Tallchief's real debut came on tour in May of 1943, when she created a role in Nijinska's *Chopin Concerto;* she repeated it at the New York premiere. Her success led to a role in *Étude*, also choreographed by Nijinska, but this abstract work danced to Bach was less popular. Tallchief worked very hard and won increasing notice, but her talent aroused the jealousy of older members of the company.

Then George Balanchine joined the Ballet Russe as ballet master. Born in Russia and trained in the Old Imperial Ballet School, Balanchine had been Diaghilev's last choreographer, then came to America in 1933. Balanchine recognized that Tallchief was ideally suited to expressing his vision. In the autumn of 1944 she created a small role in his *Danses concertantes* and a few months later, another in *Ballet Imperial*. The complexities of his choreography held no terrors for the technically brilliant Tallchief, while her rare musicality and classical purity of line helped define the Balanchine style. In 1946 Balanchine recreated *Le Baiser de la Fée* around Tallchief, and ten days later, on February 27, she created the Cocotte in his *Night Shadow*. The inspired collaboration between choreographer and dancer was sealed that same year with marriage.

The couple spent the following year at the Paris Opéra. Tallchief made her debut in *Baiser de la Fée* and was at once hailed as a ballerina of international

Maria Tallchief in *Symphony in C*

calibre. Her triumph was complete when she danced in Balanchine's classic *Apollon musagète*. Next autumn the couple were back in New York, this time with the Ballet Society, soon to become world-famous as the New York City Ballet. Balanchine continued to create roles for Tallchief, notably the leading part in *Symphonie concertante* and, later the same season, Eurydice in *Orpheus*. Tallchief was the company's prima ballerina. Although she was above all a great Balanchine dancer, her versatility appeared during guest appearances with Ballet Theatre (now A.B.T.), when she achieved outstanding success in the black swan *pas de deux*, partnered by Igor Youskevitch, and in Tudor's *Jardin aux Lilas*. On November 27, 1949 Tallchief flew onstage as Balanchine's Firebird and won phenomenal praise. A great but demanding role had found the perfect interpreter. Tallchief will always remain identified with *Firebird*, the ideal vehicle for her dazzling technique and strong temperament.

In 1960 she left the N.Y.C.B. to go on a tour of Europe and the U.S.S.R. with the A.B.T. With her regular partner, Eric Bruhn, she won international respect for the achievements of U.S. ballet. Six years later, still at the height of her powers, she retired.

Today Tallchief lives in Chicago, teaching occasional master classes. American dancers are now hailed all over the world and the excellence of U.S. ballet is internationally recognized. Maria Tallchief paved the way for this success.

Erik BRUHN

1928 - 1986

Only superlatives can begin to describe Eric Bruhn. Born in Copenhagen on October 3, 1928, at the age of nine he entered the school of the Royal Danish Ballet. There he studied the deceptively easy Bournonville tradition, the legacy of August Bournonville (1805-1879), a Danish dancer who studied with Auguste Vestris and was one of Taglioni's favorite partners. On his return from Paris he became director and choreographer of the Royal Danish Ballet, a position he held for over 35 years, during which he imparted to the company the distinctive style retained to this day. His choreography was strongly influenced by the French Romantic style he'd encountered during his early study in Paris, and his ballets are now our only link with the true Vestris manner. Despite their frequent use of Italian or Spanish settings Bournonville's ballets are characteristically Danish, full of warm, human atmosphere filled with good cheer. Moreover, the Bournonville tradition places great emphasis on the men, perhaps because he himself was a fine dancer; the *pas de deux* usually present both dancers executing the same steps, rather than the man merely lifting and supporting his ballerina. After ten years of such training Bruhn entered

Eric Bruhn in *Flower Festival at Creszaro*

the Royal Danish Ballet, becoming a soloist two years later. By then he had already danced as a guest in London and created a role in John Taras' *Designs with Strings.*

In 1949 Bruhn embarked on a career as guest artist with the major companies of the world, but primarily in America, where he danced with the A.B.T., the N.Y.C.B., and the National Ballet of Canada. At the A.B.T. he danced with Markova and later had an exciting partnership with Carla Fracci. Quickly he achieved recognition as an exceptionally strong and considerate partner. He danced all the classical *premier danseur* roles--those one-dimensional princes and counts. Bruhn's performances transformed these flimsy creatures. His immaculate technique and rare nobility of style, together with his exceptional subtlety of characterization, made these noblemen come alive. As a Bournonville dancer Bruhn has never been equalled. His James in *La Sylphide* ranks as one of the greatest performances of our time. The unusual lightness and elevation needed in Bournonville dancing and the neatness required by the small quick steps flowed from Bruhn with apparent ease and the utmost lyricism. Although he was the supreme *danseur noble,* his versatility also brought him great triumphs in modern roles, notably in Birgit Cullberg's *Miss Julie* and in Roland Petit's *Carmen.* Curiously enough, Bruhn's career included few created roles, but some of his major creations are in MacMillan's *Journey,* Cullberg's *Lady from the Sea,* and in 1962, Cranko's *Daphnis and Chloë.* Bruhn was internationally hailed as one of the world's greatest dancers until his sudden retirement in 1972.

When Bruhn returned to the theatre it was in a new role, as producer and director. For the National Ballet of Canada he directed versions of *La Sylphide* and *Swan Lake* which bore the stamp of his own remarkable intelligence and culture Bruhn then accepted the directorship of the Royal Swedish Ballet, but after four years returned to America as associate director of the National Ballet of Canada, for whom in 1975 he directed a brilliant *Coppélia,* after revitalizing Arthur Saint-Leon's classic and infusing it with his own vigor and insight. His performance as Dr. Coppélius was a masterpiece of character dancing, as was his malevolent Madge in *La Sylphide.* Bruhn also appeared again with the A.B.T., notably in the Nureyev production of *Raymonda.* Excellence marked everything he did. As a dancer he revealed new heights, bringing the male dancer once again to the fore. In his second career he revealed an equally extraordinary talent as a producer of the great ballet classics.

Rudolf NUREYEV

Born 1938

Nureyev has changed the public's image of the male dancer. His popularity has been one cause of the present growth of interest in ballet, and of the recent abundance of fine male dancers in the West. Above all, Nureyev, like all the truly great dancers of history, has enlarged and enriched ballet, revealing new possibilities of expression and technical achievement.

The first of Nureyev's extraordinary achievements was becoming a dancer at all. Of Tartar stock, he was born on a train somewhere between Lake Baikal and Irkutsk on March 17, 1938. He grew up near Ufa, amid great hardship resulting from the war and its aftermath. From childhood he loved dancing, later joining amateur folk-groups and taking tiny parts at the Ufa opera house, but his family opposed his making a career of dancing. Nevertheless, at seventeen Nureyev managed to make his way to Moscow and Leningrad, where he auditioned for the Bolshoi and Kirov schools; although he had no formal training he was accepted by both; he chose the Kirov. There he found an understanding teacher, Aleksandr Pushkin, who helped him through the difficulties caused by starting so late and by his own independent spirit. Despite constant conflict Nureyev was accepted into the company after only three years, and as a soloist. He made his debut in *Laurencia* at the special request of the Kirov ballerina, Natalia Dudinskaya. Three years later, at the last moment the authorities permitted him to accompany the Kirov on a visit to Paris, where he had a great success in *Sleeping Beauty*. This success seemed to increase the ill feelings of the Kirov authorities and so, on June 17, 1961, at Le Bourget airport in Paris, Nureyev sought asylum. His move was to change ballet in the West.

After a brief period with the Marquis de Cuevas company, Nureyev danced in London at a charity Gala organized by Fonteyn, and a remarkable partnership was born. Each brought out the best in the other, and their performances illuminated every ballet, whether through the emotional intensity unleashed or the technical brilliance revealed. Since their inspired *Giselle* in 1962 Nureyev has been a permanent guest artist with the Royal Ballet, but he soon began to dance also with all the other major companies of the West and with all the great ballerinas. He needs new worlds to conquer, and he meets each new challenge brilliantly. Although not physically ideal for them, he dances all the classical leads. Somehow he transforms himself into the perfect *danseur noble*, partnering with the utmost tenderness and consideration, and disclosing new insights in his interpretations. In the modern classics, like Fokine's *Petrushka*, Balanchine's *Prodigal Son*, or Ashton's *Fille mal gardée*, Nureyev's outstanding performances testify to unequalled versatility--he is a chameleon, capable of changing his style and line to express the choreographer's intention perfectly. He has created more, and more varied, roles than any other dancer in history. In 1975 Martha Graham created *Lucifer* for him, and he mastered

Rudolf Nureyev as *Le Corsair*

the Graham style as completely as he had done the varieties of classically-based style. He is a dancer of dazzling, exciting technique, but more important, his virtuosity always serves expressive purposes.

Nureyev's contributions to ballet includes productions of the classics; some, like Act IV of *La Bayadère* for the Royal Ballet and *Raymonda* for the A.B.T., were new to the West, while his versions of standard works revive their freshness and significance, notably his excellent, intelligent *Nutcracker* for the Royal Ballet. As a choreographer, beginning with reinterpretations of *pas de deux* from the Soviet repertory and most notably in 1977 with a new full-length *Romeo and Juliet*, Nureyev has helped bring the male dancer to prominence. In 1983 he became artistic director of the Paris Opéra Ballet, and three years later he brought the company to New York for its first visit since 1948.

Natalia MAKAROVA
Born 1940

Every generation has its great Giselle. Today's unrivalled interpreter is Natalia Makarova, born October 21, 1940 in Leningrad. She studied in the famous Kirov school, joined the company at nineteen, and soon became one of its most outstanding ballerinas. Her performances in the classical roles won praise as exceptionally fine realizations of the Kirov style, and when she first danced Giselle, at Covent Garden during a tour, she was at once recognized as a ballerina of great dramatic force as well. Despite her eminence with the Kirov, she decided, in the autumn of 1970 while the company was appearing in London, to remain in the West. This difficult decision was prompted largely by her dissatisfaction with the Kirov's arid repertory; she had danced all the major ballerina roles already, and no significant new works were being created in that stultifying atmosphere.

Makarova now began a career as a freelance dancer, first joining the American Ballet Theatre as guest artist and then also becoming guest artist with the Royal Ballet. Although the new roles to create which she considers a dancer's life-blood have been slow in coming, she was immediately offered roles new to her. She gives a touching and deeply moving portrayal as Juliet in MacMillan's *Romeo and Juliet*, and in the title role of his *Manon* she achieves an interpretation of great subtlety and insight. More surprisingly, given her training in the Kirov tradition, Makarova showed a wonderful affinity for very modern, plotless ballets, notably works by the American choreographers Jerome Robbins and Glen Tetley. In these her beautifully long line and strong, assured technique more than compensate for an often eccentric response to the music. Makarova's interpretations of the great classical roles achieve a brilliant fusion of the elegance and purity of the Kirov style with her own unique commitment to the emotion of the works. In *Swan Lake* she moves from a delicately poignant Odette, emphasised by her remarkably fluid arms and back, to a dazzling, brittle Odile, presenting a portrait of gripping power. This dramatic versatility reaches its height in her justly renowned Giselle. The mad scene is a triumph of understated expressive intensity, while in Act II she evokes a mood of mysterious, otherworldly love offering forgiveness from beyond the grave. As well as being one of the finest tragic ballerinas of the age, Makarova also possesses a fine comic gift, shown in Ashton's *Cinderella*. And by the sheer excitement of her technical accomplishments, particularly the force of her incomparable leaps, she transforms a bravura piece like the *Don Quixote pas de deux* into a memorable experience. Her dramatic and stylistic range is phenomenal. And, in the best Russian tradition, it

Natalia Makarova in *Giselle*, Act II

is supported by equally phenomenal temperament, which reached its height when a quarrel with Nureyev caused a three-year interruption of one of her most exciting partnerships. Her temperament makes her an erratic dancer; she needs the stimulus of a great partner to bring out her own genius. Ivan Nagy and that most masterful of dancers, Anthony Dowell, did this, as did her partnership with Baryshnikov, celebrated in Robbin's creation for them, *Other Dances*.

Makarova's boundless energy emerged in other spheres as well. In 1974 she staged an excellent *Bayadere* Act IV for A.B.T. and revealed a genuine talent for directing. She once said, "to be complete, woman needs child." In February, 1978, she had a son by her third husband, a San Francisco businessman. By June she was back on stage, in the demanding *Don Quixote* with A.B.T. Her return was greeted with one of the warmest welcomes ever heard, even from the enthusiastic New York audiences. Makarova's second career in the West came to a close when she retired from dancing in 1986.

Mikhail BARYSHNIKOV
Born 1948

The latest force to explode onto the American dance scene is Mikhail Baryshnikov, one of the century's most brilliant virtuosos. Mischa was born in Riga, Latvia, on January 27, 1948. His family had no connection with the theatre, but when his mother took Mischa to the local ballet, he became interested. He entered the school at Riga, but did not make the difficult decision to devote himself to the demanding art until his astonishing promise won him a place in the Leningrad school. There he studied with the great teacher Pushkin, who had been Nureyev's mentor. In 1967 he joined the Kirov, as a soloist, quickly becoming known as one of the most remarkable technicians among the young dancers. Yakobson choreographed the solo, *Vestris*, as a tribute to him, and in 1970 he created the title role in Sergeyev's *Hamlet;* the following year he created Adam in the Kirov's grandiose version of *The Creation of the World.* Despite these opportunities and his growing popularity with the public, when he visited Toronto with the Bolshoi in 1974 he chose to remain in the West. Like Makarova he sought a more varied repertory and the chance to dance in modern ballets. And like Makarova, he found these with the A.B.T.

Baryshnikov's first roles in America were in the classics with which he was already familiar. He gave notable performances in *Swan Lake* and *La Sylphide*, and as Solor in Makarova's staging of *La Bayadère* he unleashed a bravura display which only seemed the more incredible when repeated. His original combinations of breath-takingly high, light leaping steps with turns defy description--and imitation.

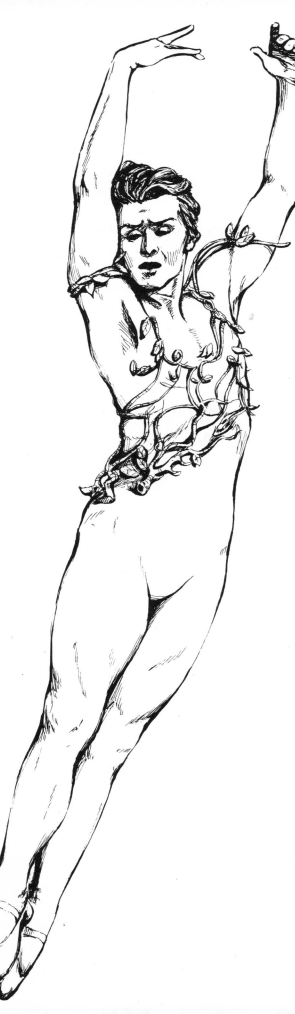

Mikhail Baryshnikov as *Auguste Vestris*

But, like most young dancers, he met the technical challenges more readily than the dramatic ones. When Baryshnikov first appeared at Covent Garden in MacMillan's *Romeo and Juliet* it was evident that he had not yet mastered the style or the emotional demands, but his return as Romeo the following season showed a great advance, testifying to his speed at learning. His Colas in *Fille mal gardée* revealed an immediate feeling for the Ashton style and a delightful comic sense. Baryshnikov recognizes that he is at his best when he has a strong rapport with his partner; his ideal partner, he declares, "is one with whom you can dance with eyes closed." For a number of years the A.B.T.'s remarkable young ballerina Gelsey Kirkland fulfilled this ideal. Within two years of his joining A.B.T., the new works he wished for began to come his way. He created the title role in Neumeier's *Hamlet: Connotations*, but not even a Baryshnikov could save that confused work from failure. A complete change of style appeared in Twyla Tharp's enormously successful *Push Comes to Shove*, which made excellent use of his comic gifts and engaging personality.

The young dancer continued to grow. On December 21, 1976 he made his debut as a choreographer with a fine version of *The Nutcracker* for A.B.T. His performance in the popular film *The Turning Point* attracted new audiences to ballet. In 1978 he joined the New York City Ballet to work with the great master of modern classicism, Balanchine. After a brief but stimulating stay he resigned to become artistic director of the A.B.T.

In 1984 he choreographed Prokofiev's *Cinderella* for the A.B.T.—the first original full-length story-telling ballet in its history.